Table of Contents

Introduction

Chapter 1

Chapter 2

Chapter 3

Chapter 4

Chapter 5

Chapter 6

Chapter 7

Chapter 8

Chapter 9

Chapter 10

Chapter 11

Chapter 12

Chapter 13

Chapter 14

Chapter 15

Acknowledgments

I would like to give a special thanks to all the women in my past who inspired me to discover how complex women have the power to be.

I would also like to acknowledge Michelle Williams, for being someone that opened my eyes and allowed me to truly shine beyond words.

Special thanks to Gregory Schley, who has a very artistic way of explaining the art of women to me, He's not always right but he's not always wrong either, and for that I'm grateful for him

Special thanks to Nathan Sanchez, who prefers women that challenge him to reach unattainable heights and measures.

Introduction

As we enter another journey of a relationship guide book let me be the first to tell you this is not your average relationship guide book. In my eyes most, relationship guide books sugar coat the real emotions that come with having a significant other, dating, and not knowing where to even start. Before discovering the difference between a thot and queen, I found myself quite confused about who to trust and who deserved my heart. It is no secret; most men and women search for the answers to the questions haunting their souls and leaving them confused in their relationships. By reading this book it will give you an upper hand and a divine insight on what you may be doing wrong or what you might be doing right in your relationship. But one thing I will guarantee you'll discover is the difference between a Thot and a Queen. Happy hunting.

Chapter 1

The Truth

The truth is women must grow to understand their worth. The same worth which empowers the heart and replenishes the soul. The same worth that raises kids and works two jobs to make ends meet. Finding that type of self-worth takes a sense of courage rooted deeply in the hearts of many women. But you must be willing to explore your inner essence to truly extract such a divine power hidden within your core. You have to be willing to reach down deep into the

depths of your heart, and pull out
something so special and true, that no
man or past insecurities can deny:
Something that will shine beyond all
stars in the nightly sky. Something
that will give you a glow only a
righteous man can view or look at. It
starts by being truthful with yourself.
What is the truth? The truth is simple.
You've accepted the lies your man has
presented to you. Why? Why did you
allow yourself to believe the lies your
man told you? Because you hoped he
would appreciate your worth. But
sadly, you discovered that issuance
has no merit in hoping someone
doesn't be little or break your heart.
Hope is for suckers!! You need
something a little stronger than hope.
You need the truth. And the truth is
good women deserve better. Better
respect, better forms of trust, better
love, better jobs, better pay, better

understanding. And most importantly better men. Its time for women to start realizing the difference between a diamond and a rhinestone. See a diamond is strong, beautiful, and worth something. When people see you with a diamond on your arm (Female: Hand), they automatically know you are important enough to have a diamond on. What does a person give another person when they desire to marry them? A diamond. (A diamond not a rhinestone).

Rhinestones are colorless imitation stones made of glass and paste. The truth is rhinestones are fake diamonds. So, if your man is messing around with a rhinestone type of female, you know why? Because he doesn't understand the difference between a diamond and a rhinestone. That's the truth.

See ladies you have to demand the truth out of your man, but even better, you have to be willing to accept the truth as well. The truth is you're beautiful and stronger than you think you are. Don't let anyone take that away from you. Demand the better things in your life. By demanding the better things in your personal life, you are granted the truth. A truth that doesn't lie to you. A truth that empowers you, gives you beauty, shows you love, honors your bond, holds you in the middle of the night, heals your pain, talks to you, makes you feel like you always should, like a DIAMOND.

"The truth will set you free"

Ladies as you read over this passage, please remember the golden rule of all relationships. "Trust." Trust is very vital in all relationships, where as some would say it is not. Let's say you have an untrustworthy mate. Every time you turn around there's some kind of messed up allegation coming out about them. This is called "dirt." And dirt must be handled accordingly to its purpose

"Sweeping the floor"

Quick question: When your floor gets dirty at home, what do you do?

You clean it right! This works the same way with your relationship. Not saying you have to do anything dramatic like break up with your mate or some crazy ritual to get your floor clean. But the truth is you need to sit down with your mate and rebuild the trust bonds. Here are two passages on trust I ask you to consider. The first one forces you to self-reflect upon your levels of trust within yourself. The second piece puts focus on how you and your mate's trust levels are compatible.

Making a list in your head, ask yourself (who do you trust?) Why or why not?

As a couple, do you trust your mate enough to hear something about them, and still believe their story? What about if your mate has cheated on you in the past? Does that make it harder to believe them?

I'm pretty sure it does, and you know why right?

Because you don't fully trust them like you would want too.

The curious part of your brain says "I don't want to be hurt any more, so before that happens I will not fully trust".

Trust is something that is earned over many years, and the more you take away from that trust bond, the less you have invested in the bank.

"Don't break the bank- you'll pay for it later"

For all the queens in a struggling relationship, where trust and the truth has become a problem. Here is a passage you can read to your mate and then ask them if they understand you and the message you just read to them, and then ask them what is there definition of trust?

In a world where everything seems to change, it is us that remains the same knowing how firm we stand on the bond we've built together, brings us joy. I know what it feels like to not have anyone to trust. It was a very troubling time in my life I'm sure you know this feeling very well to be all alone, to be misunderstood. Then you entered my life, and showed me what

it feels like, to have someone support
me, to have someone who believes in
my dreams. To hear you say "you
have my back!" To be there for me
when I need you the most. That's trust
or should I say that's us.

Chapter 2

The Lie

Alright lovely ladies of the world, I gave you the guys the truth in my last chapter, now I'm about to give your guys the lie.

What is a lie? But before you answer that question. How many times have you lied to yourself? Seriously though, if you were to think back to all the times you took a man back hoping he would treat you right and grow to love you unconditionally, is it safe to say you told yourself a lie?

I get it, and I understand why you did it. You wanted so badly to be able to change him into the man you wanted him to be. To mold him like a fine piece of clay. But be careful, because here's where the lie is told. You can't change anyone who isn't ready to change. Let me say this again (you can't change anyone who doesn't want to change.) People, including men, are just like the four seasons in life. Winter, Summer, Spring and Fall. In the winter time your man might be rough, and want to show manhood. He might desire to be treated like you want him to be, a big strong man (let him have those moments of power and feelings of conquering the world.) You're strong as well, but sometimes you have to let the bull run with the bulls ya know. He'll thank you later for it. When he's laying in your embrace, and each part of your body

seems to be on fire, he'll remember
where his power comes from.

You are the power ladies, not only
do you have the power but you are the
power.

The power of kindness and
gentleness, which only mother nature
knows. The power of lust and heart
wrenching desire. The power of
truthfulness and being openly honest.
Don't lie to yourself, and deny your
true powers ingrained in your DNA.
You are a woman, and a woman gives
life and power. A woman holds true
to such defining principles that shape,
and mold her mind frame. A woman
knows what it means to separate a lie
from the truth. And the truth is you
have to start appreciating yourselves.

Why do people lie?

I'm sure I don't have to tell you,
People lie for numerous reasons.

Some people lie to their mates because they fear the reaction of the truth. Like say if you have someone who loves you very much, but their sex game is very poor. You may lie to them in order to avoid hurting their feelings. How do you tell someone that they suck at sex? Or maybe they complain too much when you're around them. Always bringing your vibe down. You don't want to hurt their feelings by telling them every time they open their mouth they sound like Keith Sweat, complaining about something. That gets annoying real fast. Don't get me wrong, I'm not endorsing or promoting lies I'm just informing you how some people care more about not hurting people's feelings than telling the truth. Say if a woman asks me "do you think I'm getting fat?" Now I may have noticed she's been hitting the donuts pretty

hard, but I don't want to hurt her
feelings. And depending on our bond
and how well she accepts the truth, I
may lie to her. Sadly, to say,
sometimes things don't work out the
way we plan them too. That's why I
always say (a healthy dating life is
like a breath of fresh air). With a
healthy dating life, you are granted
the option to see what truly fits your
personality. You're able to be accurate
in your choosing selection of mates.
There's nothing wrong with saying
"you're a very nice person, but I don't
see a match between the two of us."
And certainly, don't allow a dating
website to pick your mate for you.
That's a little strange. Not saying a
person can't find love on a dating
website. It's just better if you trust
your own instincts on such a matter

Most people have a master degree
in BS-ing. The truth is something that

hurts, but I promise you it will set you free. That is not just a clever saying, it is the cold hard truth. State what you want right off the bat, and do not play around with emotions.

I want to tell ya'll a story about me so I use to be the grand master on this issue-King of BS-ing. Thinking I was faster than everyone, I would lie to females and twist that lie around to serve it up on a platter to another female later on. This one time I was with this woman who fell for me and I knew it. I cheated on her the first chance I got. She forgave me, but she told me "do not ever cheat on me again!" I heard her words but I did not take heed to her tone of voice as she said it. (Listen to the tone fellas). So here I did it again. Unaware that she meant every word she said. She asked me to come outside one snowy night and I did, getting in her car to sit and

talk I thought. She pulled out a 22
pistol and pointed it right at my head.
I froze as if I was dead already. She
asked me some questions under
pressure.

Like "why did you cheat on me?"

"What did I do to you to make you
hurt me?"

" Do you want to die?"

" How many women have I
cheated on her with?"

" What were their names?"

" Am I stupid if I do not shoot
you?"

She did not shoot me, but what she
did meant a lot more to me at that
time. She gave me a divine look at
how it would have felt to die over
something so stupid as hurting a
female for my own selfish greed. I
thank her for that view of sudden
death. She helped me grow.

Chapter 3
The Appreciation

Alright check this out. In the lie I spoke about how important it is not to lie to ourselves, and accept lies from men or whoever right. Then we ended with a little thing called learning how to appreciate yourselves. And that's what makes me ask the question (do you appreciate yourself?) I know what some of you might be saying to yourselves, "hell nah! I don't appreciate myself." And I'm more than happy to tell you why beautiful ladies. The reason why you don't appreciate yourselves, is because sadly to say, most of you don't know how to appreciate yourselves. Most of you don't know how to accept your beauty and bring joy to heart broken situations. Ask yourself this one question, when was the last time you bought yourself something sexy to wear? When was the last time you had a warm body massage? Or poured yourself a tall glass of red wine. Or something so simple as a steaming body bath with all the smell goods in the water. Did you turn the music on? Did your mind drift away? With no worries, no insecurities, no tears, no fears. No passing judgment on yourself, no demands, no expectations, no lies, no regrets. No let downs or disappointments...... You were truly free.

See I believe learning how to appreciate yourself makes others appreciate you as well. They always say the way you treat yourself reflects how others will treat you as well.

So, here's what I recommend all the bold diamonds of the world to do. Find a quiet time of peace, and say something beautiful to yourselves. If you can't think of anything beautiful to say to yourself remember this, I am unique in every which and way. I don't have to look like anyone but me, no man can take away from me something I don't give him. I am powerful and bold. I am worthy of being appreciated.

What is a queen? An important masterpiece, someone at peace in her own entity, someone who is shy in quiet moments loud when feeling defensive, but she handles her distress with grace, she is also in a beautiful place (mentally). She also knows how to move or be still in different situations. When to say the right things, when to use her will power. Her graceful stare can give you life or steal your air. She is strong she is knowledgeable. She is understanding, bold, and profound.

So, are you the type to hold your emotions inside, forcing your mate to pry them out of you? I use to be the type of guy who avoided certain subject matters that were hard for me to discuss. Something which helped me with this problem was talking and opening up more. Now, people who know me, say I talk too much. So, the question is do you respect your mate with your emotions? Sometimes when we grow close to a person, we tend to forget about the healthy boundaries that say (even though you are my mate I still respect you and your space.) Like for instance, many couples choose to have separate bank accounts, while other couples feel whatever is mine is yours. How does this effect your emotions with your mate? I feel every couple should talk about different situations and understand and be careful on how you respond. And when it comes to your relationship be creative, remember to spice things up don't be dull. Change it up.

In contemplation it feels as if life is passing me by. I ask why certain life lessons are paid with such higher stakes than others may reflect upon? I know the answer to my question. Certain life lessons are hard to accept simply because we make them more complex in our minds. Ask yourself: what truly makes me happy? We think we know what love feels like, since we form pictures of it in our minds during our growing moments. Unaware of the lack of depth that

entrails the entity that is love. Say you
meet someone, you feel the two of
you have a lot in common, and you
long to be around this person. You tell
yourself you admire this person. You
can't wait to be around them, or near
them every chance you get.
Everything seems to be going alright
in the relationship until something
goes wrong. A disagreement, or
differences of opinion (oh no!) Then
you fight, get mad at one another, and
say a few things to hurt/cut the other
person. Time to split up, or break up.
Not saying anyone should tolerate
abuse by far, but there is a thin line
between love and hate. The truth is
we treat love like fine china, putting it
in cabinets, afraid to eat out of it.
Treating it as if it's something inside a
display case to marvel at.

   We have to start asking ourselves
(what do we want?) Do we want to be

treated poorly? If we do, then it is best for us to embrace how others treat us as well. It's that simple.

What should love look like?

What should it feel like?

Pain. Hurt. Disappointment. Low-self esteem, Ect.

I always say struggle builds character. We live in a pancake tasting world, where no one wants to fight for everything anymore. Even our families and dear friends put limits on love. Feeling let down when such efforts aren't met or reflected.

Do you remember the first time someone said "I love you" to you?

How did you feel when hearing those magical words said to you?

Who said them to you? Your mother, your father, brother, sister, boyfriend or girlfriend. Whoever said it to you made you feel some type of way I would assume.

How about this (do you remember the first time you told someone you loved them?)

How did that make you feel? Were you nervous when saying it?

I bet it made you feel pretty good all over, right?

That is what it's supposes to feel like if you ask me. A feeling that you can have forever, good or bad.

Chapter 4
Mutual Understanding

Alright Ladies!!

This is a very important message to all the beautiful ladies out there. With all the recent news dividing people and causing scandals, it's best if we take this time to address something everyone holds dear, to their hearts, mutual understanding.

See I understand how "beautiful" women are to the world. But I also understand why women are so defensive in this day and age. Women are sick and tired of being pushed to the side, treated like play things. Over looked for promotions. Told to be quiet, and know your role. (That's some bullshit!) And I get why women are so pissed about this nonsense. It's a new era ya'll! Its time to start having grown up conversations about mutual understanding. Like understanding when your lady wants to talk and feel admired, like asking her questions to find out why she's upset, like showing your man you can be strong and hold it down ladies. Listen ladies, understand that you are beautiful, strong, trust worthy, loving, compassionate, smart, talented, successful, worthy of attention, playful but also powerful, and most importantly misunderstood. Let us understand you, and then, only then- can we grow together with mutual understanding.

As a team you conquer the world together, but you also face the same defeats. It is not your wins that will

boost your bonds but the losses.
(why?)

Anyone can win and smile it takes a different kind of person to lose and know that purpose out weighs trophies. As a couple or whatever you call yourselves, you are a team. A lean mean fighting machine. Everything you do must be as one. One mind, one body, one soul. Separate bank accounts though. Truly as said if you are not one you are two. And two rights do not make a wrong. Help out as much as possible in a relationship, ask questions. Be open, listen, look, learn and remember. Shut up, or know when to shut up. Do not get upset. Do not help too much, that is torment. Never listen to friends...Friends are stupid and they will sell your ass out fast. I'll make this very short and sweet, family can be very challenging in some relationships. You have to be careful about snares that happen or don't happen. I learned the hard way about how family has secrets in the treasure chest. You have to ask questions in order to know. Just don't get ahead of yourself, it can be tricky, stay on your guard, and remember, you and your mate are a team. Keep it tight and play it by ear.

Every couple fights. It's not the end of the world. My aunt use to say "until you start fighting, you don't know each other (the real each other) that comes out to play. Here's a little advice: the next time you guys have an argument, take control of the disagreement together. You do this by telling yourselves, (I'm not trying to win) or beat my mate in a debate. What I am saying is you don't have to be right when you an argument with your mate. Even if you are right, its

better if you win gracefully.
Remember you still care about them,
and you're not trying to hurt them.
You just want them to understand
your point of view. Here are some tips
to a healthy argument: be mindful of
the tone of your voice, get your point
across (don't yell), don't bring up old
stuff (the past is the past.) Be
understandable, listen to one another
and most of all say you love each
other when its over. These are things
you can ask your mate and yourself to
see how much mutual understanding
there is in your relationship.

If your mate was dying from a
terminal brain disease and asked you
to promise them you would pull the
plug on them if they got to sick?
Could you do it? Would you? Why?
Or why not? I honestly do not know if
I could.

If you and your mate got lost in the woods and you looked for them for 10 years how long would it take for you to give up? Be honest. "I would look for you forever my love." Liar Liar pants on fire. Remember a tree has leaves people.

Friends are like the sun. Reflecting everything that we see. Giving us a good look at ourselves and showing us who we desire to be. Sometimes they break (our minds)

but are still bright... Friends gives us light. Remember love who loves you and the haters to I guess.

Chapter 5
The Choice

Despite what many say, you have a choice when it comes to choosing a significant other. Some would consider their power of choice as the greatest strength in their emotional lives. Let's look at it from another perspective. Say you were to dine out at your favorite restaurant. A low-key spot with dim lights and beautiful jazz music. As you entertain your most inner thoughts, the menu screams for your stomach to please it gracefully. What do you have a taste for? I'm curious to find out what selection you choose. Do you even know what you want? How do you choose your mate or the people you date? Are you attracted to bad boys or squares? Would you like a pretty boy who has a slick tongue to whisper sweet nothings in your ear? Do you enjoy muscles and a six pack? Take your time when viewing the menu of connections. Why do you think we call it "M.E.N.U" or should we spell it like this Men You? As in what kind of "men" do "you" choose? Here's something to consider when choosing a mate or significant other. How does this particular person make you feel? When you're in their presence, does time seem to melt away slowly? Do they brighten every day with a royal smile? When you listen to Sade's

"No Ordinary Love", How do you feel about this person? No matter how you answer this question, just remember you have the power of choice.

Choose Wisely.

As we begin to take a personal inventory of our relationship choices, is it safe to say we deliberately over look the tell-tale signs? Why do we do that? Is it simply because we have a bleeding heart for that person? Or are we guilty of the first cardinal sin in every relationship? Trying to change someone who doesn't want to change, or isn't ready to change. I know how you feel. Stomach in knots, head aching, about to pull your hair out because the person you love the most just doesn't seem to get it. I mean you would love for your message to hit home but clearly it does not.

Tell-Tale Signs

Are you the kind of person who meets a guy/girl at the bar, flirts with them, and sleeps with them the same night?

Say if you were to have sex with a friend and two days later you refuse to call them back because you felt ashamed you crossed that line with them. How long would you wait to call them back? And how would you feel if someone did that to you?

When you attend a club, what kind of man/women do you prefer to mingle with?

Describe Here:

____

____

____

____

____

I can't tell you how many times
women have asked me about
remaining in toxic relationships, and
how to go about getting out of them.

The first thing I like to point out,
from the bottom of my heart, is
nothing good could ever come from
anything toxic. For instance: you
wouldn't take a swim in a lake of
sewage right! Then why would you
continue to dwell in a toxic situation.
No matter how much you may desire
too. I know how you feel, your mate
use to be such a nice person before
things went wrong and you might feel
slightly guilty for the outcome of your
relationship. Don't feel guilty for
something you can't change or help.
To be honest with you, giving your
toxic mate some space, could be the
best thing for you or both of you.
After you separate from the toxic
mate, you'll get a chance to see the

healthy side of your former self emerge. Toxic means poison and poison is designed to kill everything (everything). Remember when you consider yourself a queen and carry yourself in accordance to those principles, you are worth being cherished. A queen understands her true worth, and refuses to be treated less than her highest potential. A T.H.O.T has to settle for anyone she can get, even if the relationship is toxic. A queen isn't afraid to evade a toxic relationship, she knows she deserves better. A queen strives to have more and be more everyday, getting it the right way. Look at Beyonce and Michelle Obama for examples, they are true queens in the flesh, and you are as well. If you tell yourself, you are a T.H.O.T and you carry yourself in that fashion, then

others have no choice but to treat you
accordingly.

Chapter 6
How to grow your partner

Since the beginning of time, women have studied the science of partnership. What this actually means is women have spent countless centuries trying to grow the perfect man. He's a man not a plant! And despite what stereo typical non-sense you've heard, you can't grow anything or anyone who isn't ready to grow. Many women have tried to grow their partners like plants, only to find themselves frustrated, disappointed and exhausted. But you ask the question, why do women stay in relationships like those? Is it because the women who have immature partners believe their raising a child. Think about it for a minute.... By the innate natural of most women raising a child comes first hand. Sorry fellas! Women are better at raising children as a collective whole. But hear this and hear this well, you have to stop enabling your mate. When we enable our mates, we emotionally emasculate them, and stagnate any further growth they may achieve in the relationship. If we truly want to grow with our mates, we must grant them the opportunity/ability to play the role which is designated.

Communication

Regardless of what anyone thinks or says, it is evident, communication rules the nation. Everywhere you go, you see people communicating with one another. Well they use to communicate more with one another before cell phones turned everyone into digital zombies. None the less, the power of communication is well needed and very important in our day to day lives. One of the strongest ways to have a healthy relationship with your mate or if you simply want to extract information out of them, just pick a form of communication.

-What are some forms of communication-

Verbal communication is a way of life for all humans. It is an art form, which paints vivid pictures to the mind. There are actual classes you can take to strengthen your verbal communication skills

Body language is the movements (being hands, feet, lips and posture) in which your mate demonstrates as communication. If their feet are moving too much it means they are anxious to go somewhere or be somewhere probably to get away from your ass. Now this does not always mean they're cheating on you or anything like that, they could be very anxious to go to a friend's house to watch the playoffs. No matter what the outcome may be, its best you know how important body language is in your relationship.

Active listening is the art of listening without judgment. You have to sit there and truly be engaged in what your mate is conveying to you. Don't drift off into wonderland, thinking about what you're going to

cook for Thanksgiving dinner.
Actually, listen to what your mate is
saying to you. Listen to what kind of
words they are using, and how they
use them. Fight back the urge to speak
or interject your own thoughts.

Chapter 7
Building Bond

If we take a bird's eye view of most relationships, we would probably agree with one word "building". When you are building with your mate, you find yourself leaving the you-factor out of it, and adopt the we factor.

What is the we factor?

The we factor is where you and your mate are comfortable spending time together. You begin the building process, one block at a time.

Don't worry about how it looks at first, just start building. You might even have to rediscover one another again, ask questions, find out what they look like now (it might have changed). Just remember if the building was worth designing, and creating it has value. Anything that has value is always worth repairing. Also remember part of working on yourself, surely helps enhance the relationship. It makes you stronger when you know your triggers, and when you study your mate's triggers as well.

"Every great architect knows each and every corner of the building it's what they do best"

Someone once told me "a mate is a mate and a friend a friend." When I heard this, I was alarmed saying to myself, "my mate can't be my friend as well?" Surely, I disagree, see to understand us a person must know what it feels like to be close to an angel. To be able to hang out with your mate and have true fun with them. To laugh with them, and hold their hand in the park. To share secrets with them and open up your heart to them. To have them trust you, and support your dreams. Nothing should mean nothing more than to build this bond with your mate. To say "my mate is my best friend, and we do everything together" while we watch other couples try to make friends with other people, unaware of their mate is their best friend.

No matter how old you become, it's best to keep the spice in your relationship, no one wants to be in a dry ready-made relationship. Just like no one wants to eat rice cakes all the time. That would simply suck. Don't be afraid to add a little spice to your relationship. How? Say if you always go to the same restaurant after church on Sunday. You find yourself at the same bar on Wednesdays. You do all the same stuff all week long (word of advice) you're not a robot so stop acting like one. Change it up every now and then, it won't hurt you to step out on faith.

"If you put yourself in a dog cage everyday, don't be shocked when people try and pet you".

It has been a proven fact, mates who work out together develop a stronger bond. Not saying you have to be some power lifting couple you see on TV or a gladiator, but it does stir up good companionship between you and your mate. Most women I talk to, always ask me about how they can get closer to their mate? I always tell them, in order to build a heavy bond with your mate, you have to get to know them. Of course, your mate has to get to know your likes and dislikes as well. The power of the queen, over throws the ideas of the T.H.O.T.

Repeat after me, I will not let a T.H.O.T take my man, and if he can't cherish my inner essence than do away with his ass.

Chapter 8
Remember

As we take a reminiscing look at all women had to endure in everyday life, we can't help but be astonished. Women have over come feats beyond imaginable circumstances. This is true, but here's the puzzling question jogging through the minds of most men and women, "where did the world go wrong telling young women and girls its alright to be a T.H.O.T?" Let's explore this notation in full beautiful ladies. Remember how your grandmothers were. They were as the independent women of today are; strong, smart, wealthy, beautiful, loving and truly unique. They defied the odds of traditional set backs and consternation times. Think about what it means to be a super hero or someone young girls can inspire to be like. I envision my own grandmother as I write this to you, who showed me a lot of attributes. I see in the strong lovely ladies of today's times (power, skill, honor, compassion, truth, intelligence. and alternating change).

By taking a bold step into the future of womanhood, we are granted the pleasure to see doubt and despair kicked to the curb. That's right beautiful queens of the world, It's a new day. But just out of curiosity, what are some of the things that cause doubt and despair?

(Job, kids, weight loss. Being accepted by others, going back to

school, or finding love.) I would
guess these following things have
haunted countless of women over the
years. But why do beautiful women
allow certain things to get underneath
their skins? Don't they see what I see?
Don't they understand what it means
to be bold and beautiful? Here's my
advice if you care to hear it. Every
time doubt or despair creeps into your
head or your heart, replace those
thoughts with positive reassuring
thoughts. By doing that you'll create a
healthy balance that allows you to
engage the things you should be
worrying about, and the things you
should let go. Remember how strong
you are, and all the things you've over
came. Trust me, it helps to remember
those things

Chapter 9
Cheaters never win....
Or do they?

Am I the only one who feels like sometimes it doesn't pay to do the right thing in a relationship? Seriously though, how many times have you been faithful to someone who you believed would never break your heart eyes out, trying to figure out what you did wrong? The answer you are looking for could be nothing at all. You can't go around blaming yourself when other people cheat on you. That's a fact. Here's how you should look at it if you ask me. If you know you are a good person in your heart, no one can take that away from you.

Also, if you know you are loving, caring, compassionate, smart, beautiful, and well off, then you must know you are what we call a diamond. And diamonds never lose value, they only gain value (no matter who's wearing them.)

Vulnerability: I knew this female a few years ago who would do something very odd to me. She would fall head over heels for a guy, and give her entire heart and soul, instantly. A couple of months later the same guy would break her heart, only you have them trample over your feelings like a dirty rag? That sucks, right!! Someone once told me a long time ago, cheaters never win, I ask "do they?" We feel this way because we ask ourselves, how could someone hurt us when we did nothing or said anything to bring this about. You sit at home, crying your leaving her in a state of depression. Then I would see her in the club getting sloppy drunk and going home with random guys. Not saying I was all in her business like that, but she had a reputation as being what many men call as an easy score. She would then find another guy who she thought was the one, only to repeat the process over and over again. What I took from her circle of pain was the fact she reacted to her vulnerability in a way which caused more pain. She went from being full of life, to having an empty lifeless stare in her eyes. Have you ever done something you regretted in the morning? How did you feel about doing it? What are some lessons you've learned the hard way? And how would you help your daughter or a young girl who is creating the same pattern as the woman in the story?

Value: If you were to strip yourself down, and stand in front of a full framed mirror, what about yourself would you dislike? I got a better question for you, what would you desire to change? So many times, do we find ourselves unable to discover the true value within our inner cores. Telling ourselves we're not good enough to have high standards or maybe if you enhance your breast, lips, ass, legs, or whatever else it will make you more desirable to others. And yeah men maybe fascinated at your assets at first, but gradually as time progresses, you'll see the loss of interest sink in. Why do you think that happens? Because men are fascinated with the chase, that's why we like cars so much. Not only that, men only respect things that hold value toward its worth. So, say if a woman sleeps around and gives it up as easy as

ordering take out food from a fast
food restaurant, her assets go from
being a delicacy to a dine and dash.
Sadly, to say, it loses its special
power. It loses its power of dainty. As
you explore what makes you unique,
it's best to discover your true worth as
stated before. Then and only then are
you granted the true opportunity to
see how valuable you are. You know
how they say "you don't know you
had a good thing until its gone!"
That's true. That also goes for you as
well, as stated "sometimes you have
to know you're a good thing and not a
play toy." If you act like a play toy,
boys will treat you like a play toy.
And what happens every year? A new
toy comes out! Which means you get
pushed to the side or thrown in the
closet for later. You don't have to do
that to yourselves, you're better than
that right! Some are and some just

aren't because they refuse to be better.
They'd rather be easy and hollow,
than hard and full. Recognize your
value ladies before someone tells you
it's not worth anything.

Chapter 10
The pregnancy trap

Its no secret, "you are not the father!" The crowd "Gasps" as an overly weaved headed female jumps up and runs back stage. A speechless spectacle many might say. Here's the irony moment, she has been intimate with so many partners the months of conception are a fog to her. Here you circle one:

T.H.O.T or NOT

To all the beautiful ladies of the world you can't tell me this does not upset you a little bit. Seriously though, tell me when you see a fellow female showing her ass it doesn't piss you off. I bet it does. I knew this guy by the name of Alex M. back in the day, a real smooth type of player. One of his greatest gifts was the ability to be an over all around athlete. The reason why I bring him up is to highlight a point. The moment he was getting scouted by major universities to play college ball multiple females started shouting they were pregnant with his baby. He had them all tested, only one was telling the truth. (It's a cold game baby!) Do you know any females whose ever tried the pregnancy trap with a guy? If so, would you inform the guy if you knew?

Gold Digger: I have to be honest with you guys by saying I didn't know what a T.H.O.T was at first. It came

to my notice in the form of a young
lady who stood beside me in a late-
night club I was attending. We both
happen to be watching a group of
thirsty looking females trying to
thread their way pass security so they
could stampede the V.I.P section.
Apparently, there were some football
players back in the V.I.P section, and
the "juice boxes", another name the
young lady standing next to me yelled
out loud "you juice boxes!" To
elaborate a "juice box" symbolize
how thirsty a female looks or carries
herself. It is also a reference which
takes a shot at the level capacity of
thinking many of them have (child
like minds) get it? Nonetheless I was
educated by a woman who see
T.H.O.Ts as a disgrace to womanhood
all over the world. That's when I
discovered a revelation to heart, a
curious one. I began to question a lot

of the previous females of my past.
Were they queens or T.H.O.Ts ? Little
did I know my answers would emerge
from the depths of many emotions
long stored away.

Chapter 11
Fake Friends

Have you ever heard the saying "keep your friends close and your enemies closer?" That rings truth when we speak of fake friends. Plenty women ask me the question, " how do I know I can trust my best friend around my man?" Here's a little advice to run with. If you have to ask if you can trust anyone, no matter what the relationship may be, there is no relationship. As we grow to surround ourselves around the people we say we love, it is mindful to explore the possibility of them causing us hurt. That hurt could come in the form of your best friends sleeping with your man. Some people reading this may already know the pain of having a friend or family member betray your trust. Call me crazy but the other day I was watching this reality show that had me laughing but also thinking. On the show there were these female cousins who slept with the same man. One of the cousins started dating the guy and eventually they were to be married. In true T.H.O.T life fashion, the guy sleeps with the other cousin two weeks before the wedding. (How you like them apples?) Comically as they stood on stage calling each other hoes and any other god forsaken name they could muster up, I begin to think to myself. After about 30 to 40 minutes I came up with this question to explore. What is it about females and friends who want their man? Clearly, we understand the deeper essence of finding true love when the time is right. We're not challenging that notion in the least way. What I'm saying is women are sometimes jealous of another women's happiness. There I said it. And you women of the world know I'm telling the truth. Think about it, the moment the female cousin on the reality show was engaged to be married, here comes the T.H.O.T to steal away her happiness. Not saying she's all the blame out of this whole equation, because the boyfriend looked real stupid begging his fiancé to take him back after sleeping with her cousin. (You think!)

I'm just addressing the fact, her cousin didn't even want the guy, as it would seem. She actually stated "I slept with her man because she thinks she all that!" (Hurt People-Hurt other people right!) That's when I drew the conclusion, some females like to steal other females thunder. They love to see the other female crying with snot bubbles coming out of her nose. It brings some of them pure pleasure to say "that's why I slept with your man!" They're in fact that they reached inside another woman's body and completely snatched out her heart. Isn't that some sick shit? Seriously though. That's like walking up to a baby crib and snatching the pacifier out of the baby's mouth, just so the baby will cry. Then when someone asks you why you did such an evil act, you reply "because that baby thought it was all that!" Tell me that doesn't paint a picture for the human soul to explore. And I know what could be defended about fake friends. How do you know a person is a fake friend? I refer you back to the tell-tale signs we tend to ignore. (See chapter 5) indeed, no one knows if a friend or family member will betray them (true), but sometimes there are tell-tell signs. You just have to be keen enough to recognize these signs. For instance, jealousy toward what you have, say, or do. If your friend or family member states in a jokingly manner, " I hate the fact you can eat anything and stay skinny!" Trust me when I tell you, behind every joke there is a certain level of truth hidden deep within. My advice would be stay paranoid. Don't let your guard down. The T.H.O.T is always planning and plotting to steal something from you.

It could be your diamond bracelet or it could be your man.

Chapter 12
Hit or Miss

Listen Ladies of the world, I'll make this short and sweet. If you let a guy hit it too soon, he will not respect you. Call it what you may, but it's the truth. I know what you're saying "guys do it all the time!"

"Why can't I do it!"

" That's a double standard!"

Yeah! Yeah! Yeah! I get what you're saying, but hear me out when I say this loud and clear. I don't care how much the world changes or we desire to see it change. Some things are as they always will be, if something/anything comes to easily to

anyone, it is not respected the same
way if you have to work a little harder
for it. (That's life!) Plain and simple.
Why do you think kids who were born
rich have such a hard time finding
their own path in life? Because
they've never worked for anything, it
was given to them on a silver platter.
So just to highlight my point further
I'll say, if you let anyone hit it without
effort don't be surprised if when you
go to find them, they're missing. In
baseball you hit the ball and take off
running right!

Scandalous

In modern day society we've
witnessed a massive collection of
tycoons fall from grace. Sexual
misconduct has become as normal as
your morning coffee. Every time you
turn on the TV it's some kind of

scandal smeared across your screen.
This is a very sensitive subject which
demands the nations attention from
understanding perspective. But for the
sake of this book there's another
sensitive subject that gets over
looked. It's called false claims, or in
better words destroying someone's
life. Too many times we've seen the
likes of false claim rape allegations
and sexual misconduct destroy
people's lives. Once the investigation
proves the man is innocent, there's
little understanding on such a
scandalous matter. (What the hell is
that about?) Have we grown so numb
to the fact, anybody can do some
scandalous non-sense and we take off
running. When we take a grand view
at how this plays out, are we wrong
for calling these T.H.O.T liars out. I
know what you might be saying, its
not right to blame people either. No

matter what we say, blaming others
for stuff they didn't do is wrong. And
it's very scandalous

Chapter 13
Who's motivated by money

Everyone motivated by money listen up. Do not let money issues control your life. Mates, if your significant other makes more money than you do not get upset. Do not feel less of a person. Support them the same way you would like to be supported. Be on there side. It is the two of you against the world. The same world that has changed how women are seen, treated, and understood (about time!) Remember anyone can have a service woman, but only real men desire a partner in love. When your mate comes home surprise them with a home cooked meal or order some take out. Be strong for your mate. Why? Even though your mate is making more than you doesn't mean they don't need you. The greatest turn on for any mate is someone who can be confident in their position. You do not have to always be the quarterback in order to secure a win. Do whatever you want as long as you remember your mates needs. Here is what woman will not tell men (they really do not care about money.) Not so fast ladies! Now let's say you have the power or you think you do, you make the money and your man doesn't, remember money is not power. It is not even real to be honest with you. Do not lose your man because you have money issues. Remember other women have money too, and he will go see how much they are trying to give away along with other things. Power is a very tricky element that most people are not prepared to accept. I saw this program where a football player lost a lot of money because his wife took it. She said she did it because she did not feel safe money wise, so she stashed her a little something for later. Do you blame her? Or hate her for being low-down? Discuss this issue with your mate. Ask: how much money would it take to separate us? If money continues being a problem for you and your mate it might be a good idea to get separate bank accounts. Do not feel bad about it, couples do it all the time. It is the smart couple who knows their perks and smirks. Remember as I said money is not real, no mate can stand up to money, it is

an allure that will destroy your home.
I promise you that.

Chapter 14
Love Songs

Have you ever taken the time to question what love beyond a word is? I ask this question because to know something is provides certain insights that help us master its existence. For instance, we know that there are different entities of love ranging from. Unconditional, familial, infatual, and logical. The defining factors of these emotions stem from the likes of experiences. Unconditional love is what a parent or caregiver has for a child. Many people say that unconditional love is suppose to be natural or unlearned but I disagree with that notion partially. To practice a person must experience even a glimmer of illustration. For ex: A mother that never had a mother could supersede her mental expectations, and actually become a great mother. Ex: A father who had a good father could despise the perfect nature of his father and become the complete opposite. (Go figure huh!) Speaking of family, familial love is what a sibling or someone closely related to your blood line would receive. Familial love is often conceived as the obligation to take on the undo liberties for the greater good of the family tree. We do it simply because we know the reflection of there actions and thought portrays are actions and thoughts as well. (Negative or Positive.) For example, the uncle that is a doctor or the aunt that is a federal judge brings sure joy to the family. The family is very proud and quick to say "my uncle is the best doctor in the city". The reflection of their uncle/family member being a doctor is perceived as the badge of honor to the entire family. Quick question: how many family members of convicted serial killer John Wayne Gacey brag about the likes of his actions? Infatual love is truly the most dangerous kind because the nature of thinking is absent verses the complement of attraction being present. Infatuation is defined as the appetite of an apex predator hunting for a prey in the mist. The funny thing about an appetite is once the satisfaction had been cured the need to feed goes away temporarily which conveys to the relationship getting an adieu until the urge is needed again. Logical love is valid reasoning based on earlier, or other wise known statements, events, or conditions. Most logical love is done or simply applied because of likes of money or power. For example: the love for money made kings marry princess back in the day for power. If her father was someone of great statue or influenced he would agree to unite the two families for the greater good of royalty. (Not love but royalty.) Most celebrities in this day in age marry in the act of modest modus vivendi (meaning a way of life/a manner of living.) That's probably where the word modest comes from, the acts of the public eye chooses the mate for you. If a person is not up to the likes of the public's approval the relationship automatically discredited. For

example: R/B singer Angie Stone
stated that her relationship with

D' Angelo didn't fit the mode of
the public eye." What she was saying
shines a light on this passage by
pointing out how the media has the
power to influence or put a large
amount of pressure on the celebrity to
do the (logical) thing.

I wrote all this to say I wasn't
completely aware of love, I didn't
know what it existed of, or what it
demanded, what it needed to be
whole, or how selfish it can be at
times. I know now that love means
making mistakes in order to become a
natural at it. It means loving
whomever as if the obligation was
never offered again. It means you
grow to understand the elements of its
existence by learning lessons that you
can look back on from time to time
and say you were inspired by your

faults. It means your mind, body, and your entire entity longs to explore, desire, and accept the attributes of love.

Now ladies let's be honest when approaching this word "love". I'm not certain but I'm pretty sure most millennials are scratching their heads like "what is love?" That curious question alone gives birth to what I believe is the problem in most day to day relationships. No-one knows the true definition of love. It sounds odd I'm sure, but let's dig a little deeper to discover the bold truth. First and foremost, we have to admit R&B is dead. This is very important to point out, seeing how are era of love has no driving force of affection. Or better yet there are very few reminders of true love. If we dare take a glimpse back into our grandparents' day and time, we are granted to privilege to understand why Etta James sung "At Last." She's singing about how she has found love finally, through all the bullshit, and nonsense, its her time. Can you relate to a time when you've waited for love, only to discover this person is not the one for you? Imagine if you did find that special one, how would it feel? Alright I have another moving classic for you, Lenny Williams "Cause I Love You." Now this is one of the greatest love songs of all time. The power in his voice, the raw emotion, it all gives you a sense of how deep his love was for whomever moved his heart. I seriously ask you all to truly contemplate the measurements of love, then challenge yourselves to explore what it means to donate your entire heart to someone. As you carry yourself like a true queen what does it mean to have your heart filled with

love? What does it mean to have
someone sacrifice their life for you?
To support you when no one believes
in any of your ideas. To grow with
you and ask you questions to get to
know you better, with high hopes of
understanding you more. To feel pain
when you feel pain, cry when you cry.
Refuse to lie to you, no matter how
hard the truth may seem. To be by
your side when you are broke, and
help you build an empire from the
ground up. To think about you during
the day. To worry if you're alright
throughout the night. To forgive you
when you mess up. To praise you
when you do good and be enthusiastic
for you. I got a great love song for
you, Jagged Edge "gotta be." That's a
cold-blooded love jam right there. I
call that the skating rink song, if you
know what that means. None the less,
the main subject we're harping on is

the fact that love songs are the music behind our daily relationship. If you were to ask a T.H.O.T what does the word love mean, what kind of answer would you receive? For all my queens reading this passage, think back to a time when a certain song touched your heart, and write down how you felt about it.

____

____

____

____

____

____

____

____

____

Chapter 15
The Breakdown

As we explore the attributes and qualities separating a queen and a T.H.O.T, we are asked to define the difference between the two. One of the first things I noticed about a queen was how she carried herself, and how she thought. A queen conducts herself in a proper manner, like she's supposed to not because someone holds her to a public standard. A queen has ideas, in which grow to be dreams that catapult her into a successful enterprise. A T.H.O.T sets low goals and refuses to see the true potential within self. Allowing others to live a prosper life, while never comprehending the avenue or the road needed to travel to get there, a T.H.O.T is scandalous and deceitful, forming lies around her everyday life. While a queen demonstrates a moral compass in her daily adventures. Showing young women/girls what it means to stand firm on values, principle, and past reflections. A queen demonstrates strength in her posture, in the way she speaks, and in the way, she views others. A T.H.O.T is limited to a certain thought simply because what governs her mind is surfaced. A T.H.O.T chooses to be a bottom feeder with low standards, asking why she gets treated different than the queen. The queen is respected like an eagle and the T.H.O.T gets treated like a chicken head. A queen is honored like a symbol that demands prestige expectations. While a T.H.O.T, no matter the age, gets disrespected and overlooked. A T.H.O.T embarrasses a queen when seen in public, stereotyping women as hoes, loose gooses, and bed jumpers. Unaware that women are rare, beautiful, desired, honored, loved, precious, strong, smart, open hearted, and divine. In this day and age, you must continue to fight the good fight that demands womanhood survive and era of T.H.O.T-ness. Only then will we see a generation of queens emerge from the depths of the Shadows to claim their graceful titles called beautiful women.

BIO

It's no secret, the mystery behind a thot and a queen is finally revealed. Johnathan Walker breaks down relationships, dating, friends with benefits, gold diggers, and why love is such a complicated emotion. This straight forward approach is well-needed to highlight the inner workings of a thot and a queen. Read at your own risk, but ask yourself: do you know the difference between thot and a queen

About the Author

Johnathan Walker Magnetizes the minds of many with his straight forward approach toward relationships. After solidifying himself as a motivating mentor, he grew to challenge himself in multiple areas of career counseling. Don't judge a book by its cover is his favorite saying. As a young man, he found himself forced to define the true essence of a queen. To contact Johnathan Walker his email is walker90.jw@gmail.com